D0844169

The Constitutional Amendments

The Constitutional Amendments

By William Loren Katz and Bernard Gaughran

Illustrated with Contemporary Prints and Photographs

←A FIRST BOOK→

Franklin Watts, Inc., New York, 1974

This book, conceived for use in conjunction with textbooks or encyclopedias, does not contain the text of the amendments.

All photographs and prints from the William Loren Katz Picture Collection, except painting opposite page 1, courtesy of the Smithsonian Institution.

Cover design by Terry Fehr

Library of Congress Cataloging in Publication **Data**

Katz, William Loren.
The constitutional amendments.

(A First book)
SUMMARY: Explains each of the twenty-six amendments to the Constitution.
Bibliography: p.
1. U.S. Constitution—Amendments—Juvenile literature. [1. U.S. Constitution—Amendments] I. Gaughran, Bernard, joint author. II. Title.
KF4557.K38 342'.73'03 73-14794
ISBN 0-531-00813-4

Printed in the United States of America
6 5 4 3 2

Contents

The Constitutional Amendments

For Nellie

What Is an Amendment?

To understand what a Constitutional amendment is, one should first know that the Constitution itself is the basic law of our nation. Passed in 1787, the Constitution set up the fundamental rules for the whole United States. Perhaps you have heard someone say, "That's unconstitutional!" He means that one cannot do that, because something that violates the Constitution cannot legally be done. But the Constitution still allows for quite a bit of freedom.

Constitutional amendments provide part of that freedom. The men who drew up the Constitution knew that even this basic set of rules would have to be changed as times changed. They set up a system for changes called amendments to the Constitution. An amendment is added to the Constitution to make it more modern and more workable in the present day. Since many things have changed since 1787, amendments have been used to change the Constitution as well.

How are amendments made? First, the amendment must be proposed. The constitution tells us that amendments shall be proposed "... whenever two-thirds of both Houses [of Congress] shall deem it necessary, or,

A painting by L. B. Stearns of the 1787 Constitutional Convention in Philadelphia, Pennsylvania. George Washington, the presiding officer, addresses the meeting; Benjamin Franklin is seated on the left, holding a cane; and James Madison is standing in the center. The Constitution of the United States, drafted at this convention held from May 25 to September 17, remains the world's oldest written constitution that is still being used.

on the application of the legislatures of two-thirds of the . . . States. . . ." The amendment must then be ratified; that is, passed. If three-fourths of the states ratify it, the amendment is a part of the Constitution of the United States.

Amendments are difficult to pass because it has been felt that the Constitution should not be changed for minor reasons. If it were changed frequently, no one would respect it. However, the Constitution can change and it actually has changed twenty-six times in its history. The men who drew up the Constitution planned to make change possible if the American people really wanted it. This way, they could have a strong government, but one that could change without revolution.

Enforcement

The idea behind proposing and passing any law or amendment is that it must be enforced. People who violate a law must be brought to justice. If this does not happen, the law means nothing. A rule that is generally disobeyed is not really a rule, except in someone's mind.

We all know that laws are violated and that the guilty are sometimes not brought to justice. Unfortunately, this has even happened with amendments to the Constitution of the United States. For long periods of time, some amendments have actually been regarded by the people as "dead letters," or unenforced ideas. When this goes on, imagine what happens to people's respect for the Constitution or pride in their country! How would you feel if a Constitutional amendment gave you the right to vote, and yet you were actually stopped from voting by the government of your own state? This has really happened to millions of people!

Obviously, an amendment is no good unless it is enforced. An amendment is usually short, and it is stated in fairly general language. To enforce or carry out the amendment, Congress has to pass additional laws that set up the procedures, regulations, or agencies the amendment needs if it is to work. Then it is up to the president and the courts to make sure it is enforced. If necessary, government agents or even troops can be used to make the enforcement take place. Of course, when most Americans do not support an amendment, it can be difficult or nearly impossible to enforce it. This happened with the amendment outlawing alcoholic beverages. But even the best amendment, an amendment that strengthens our democracy, an amendment that most Americans believe in, even this amendment will not work unless the government that created it stands behind it.

The First Ten Amendments: The Bill of Rights

The Constitution of the new United States of America was ratified five years after the little country had won its freedom from England. The former mother country could no longer send its tax collectors to America, or send troops with or without warrants to investigate, search, and arrest American people. No longer would any British governor forbid assemblies to meet, or suppress a newspaper, or punish citizens for collecting signatures on a petition. British suppression of our rights was ended when we ended British rule of our country.

However, the things the British had done were not easily forgotten. Americans had fought and died for rights that the mother country had abused. Might not America's own new government abuse those same rights if it became too strong? Thomas Jefferson thought it would, and he said so. Even an American government, if it were strong enough, could suppress newspapers, prevent assemblies from meeting, or punish people for circulating petitions or speaking against the government. And yet the Constitution for the new country said nothing about protecting these very rights from abuse by the American government.

George Mason of Virginia wrote a "Bill of Rights" defining the basic rights of American citizens. Although the Constitution did not mention such rights, it was ratified because the addition of these rights was promised. This promise was kept, and in 1791 the Bill of Rights — or the first ten amendments to the Constitution — was ratified.

Originally, the Bill of Rights prohibited the federal government from interfering with the rights it set forth. Later, however, the Fourteenth Amendment was passed and the Bill of Rights was extended to include the states as well. It is the phrase "due process of law" in the Fourteenth

Amendment that the Supreme Court has interpreted as meaning that states are also bound by the Bill of Rights. Today, citizens' rights are protected from federal, state, and local lawmakers.

CAN'T AFFORD
TO
WEAR PANTS
PA WORKS IN
AN OPEN SHO

The First Amendment

Americans are proud of the First Amendment to the Constitution, and they have a right to be. In a single sentence of less than fifty words, it spells out the basic rights of all Americans. Congress shall not violate these rights: freedom of religion; freedom of speech, and the press; and the right to attend meetings, form any kind of political organization, and circulate petitions.

Freedom of Religion

The first part of this amendment forbids Congress to establish a state religion; that is, a government-supported religion. The founding fathers remembered that England had supported the Anglican Church, and this led to the persecution of members of other religions. They remembered that whether Englishmen were Anglican or not, their taxes went to pay for the Anglican Church. Even many Englishmen had fought this practice, and the Americans wanted no part of it.

The First Amendment also forbade Congress to pass laws that would interfere with religious practice in any way. There were many different religions in the United States in 1787, and there are many more today. The government cannot pass laws regulating these religions. It cannot, for example, pass laws regulating their church services, or their prayers, or the qualifications of their clergymen. Thus, by keeping the govern-

This young man is expressing his opinions, an action that is protected by the First Amendment.

Above, in the Massachusetts Bay Colony members of the Society of Friends (Quakers) were executed for their religious beliefs. The First Amendment sought to protect religious minorities. Right, Eugene V. Debs, a famous socialist leader, found that all speech is not free. He was arrested, tried, and imprisoned for a speech opposing World War I.

ment out of religion, this amendment allows Americans to have complete freedom of choice in religious practice.

Why did the Supreme Court interpret the First Amendment to mean that public school prayers were unconstitutional? Public schools are paid for with the taxes of all Americans, whether they belong to this or that religion, or to no particular religion. Scheduling any prayer in public schools would mean government support of that prayer. The children whose religion did not permit them to say that prayer would have to sit or stand in silence during the prayer, or leave the room. The children who did not belong to any religion would have to do the same thing. Meanwhile, the other students would recite the government-supported prayer, or, in effect, participate in a kind of government-supported religion. However, the First Amendment forbids the government to establish a religion.

Freedom of Speech and the Press

Patrick Henry's speeches for liberty moved the colonists to a greater understanding of their right to be independent of England. When they finally secured that freedom through a hard-fought revolution, they were determined not to lose it, not even to their own American government. Therefore, the First Amendment forbade Congress to pass laws "... abridging the freedom of speech."

Government in America simply cannot tell a person what he or she may say. It cannot prohibit someone from saying something, even if no one agrees with it. An individual may explain personal viewpoints in any way he or she wishes. A person may advocate a change in government, or the firing of a president. A person may urge that all of his or her political enemies be immediately shipped to the South Pole.

Nevertheless, there are some limitations on the freedom of speech. An individual may not offer his or her viewpoint on a loudspeaker at midnight in a residential neighborhood. The right of people to privacy, or in this case to sleep, must be respected. However, a permit can be secured

Modern communications media have presented many new problems to courts seeking to protect constitutional rights.

to speak in that neighborhood at times when it does not interfere with the rights of others. Local permits are often required for speakers, and they must be granted unless the speaker would somehow violate the rights of other people. Police may patrol the area near the speaker to make sure that traffic moves, and to defend the rights of the speaker. If someone forcibly tried to remove the speaker, the police would have to protect that speaker. This can be difficult to enforce when some members of a crowd and even some policemen deeply resent what a speaker may be saying.

While the First Amendment protects the citizen's right to say anything, the Supreme Court has pointed out that certain things may not be said in certain situations. For example, a person may not falsely shout "Fire!" in a crowded theater. People would panic and lives might be lost. A lecturer may say that the government will probably never improve and may have to be forcibly overthrown. The same lecturer may not, however, urge a street crowd in Washington, D.C., to immediately attack and burn down the nearby Capitol Building. In short, a person may advocate anything, but may not incite people to commit specific, unlawful acts. It is difficult for the courts to draw the line between these different situations, but it is important and necessary that it be done.

The earliest Americans were as concerned with freedom of the press as with freedom of speech. Newspapers were very popular in colonial America, and editors and writers played an important part in explaining the necessity for separation from England.

Before the American Revolution, an historic victory for press freedom was won by John Peter Zenger, a German immigrant and newspaper editor who was living in New York. In his *Weekly Journal* he exposed the corruption of the British colonial governor, and found himself arrested. The charge against him was "seditious libel": not only was Zenger slandering the governor's character and reputation, but by criticizing a governmental official, he also seemed to be promoting discontent with the government. This charge landed him in jail for ten

A brief Narrative of the Caſe and Tryal of *John Peter Zenger*, Printer of the *New-York weekly Journal.*

AS There was but one Printer in the Province of *New-York*, that printed a publick News Paper, I was in Hopes, if I undertook to publiſh another, I might make it worth my while; and I ſoon found my Hopes were not groundleſs: My firſt Paper was printed *Nov.* 5*th*, 1733. and I continued printing and publiſhing of them, I thought to the Satisfaction of every Body, till the *January* following; when the Chief Juſtice was pleaſed to animadvert upon the Doctrine of Libels, in a long Charge given in that Term to the Grand Jury, and afterwards on the third *Tueſday* of *October*, 1734. was again pleaſed to charge the Grand Jury in the following Words.

‘ *Gentlemen*; I ſhall conclude with reading a Paragraph or two out of the
‘ ſame Book, concerning Libels; they are arrived to that Height, that they
‘ call loudly for your Animadverſion; it is high Time to put a Stop to them;
‘ for at the rate Things are now carried on, when all Order and Government
‘ is endeavoured to be trampled on; Reflections are caſt upon Perſons of all
‘ Degrees, muſt not theſe Things end in Sedition, if not timely prevented? Lenity,
‘ you have ſeen will not avail, it becomes you then to enquire after the Of-
‘ fenders, that we may in a due Courſe of Law be enabled to puniſh them.
‘ If you, *Gentlemen*, do not interpoſe, conſider whether the ill Conſequences
‘ that may ariſe from any Diſturbances of the publick Peace, may not in part,
‘ lye at your Door?

‘ *Hawkins*, in his Chapter of Libels, conſiders three Points, 1*ſt*. *What ſhall*
‘ *be ſaid to be a Libel.* 2*dly*. *Who are lyable to be puniſhed for it.* 3*dly*. *In what*
‘ *Manner they are to be puniſhed.* Under the 1*ſt*. he ſays, §. 7. *Nor can there be*
‘ *any Doubt, but that a Writing which defames a private Perſon only, is as much*
‘ *a Libel as that which defames Perſons intruſted in a publick Capacity, in as much*
‘ *as it manifeſtly tends to create ill Blood, and to cauſe a Diſturbance of the publick Peace;*
‘ *however, it is certain, that it is a very high Aggravation of a Libel, that it tends to*
‘ *ſcandalize the Government, by reflecting on thoſe who are entruſted with the Admini-*
‘ *ſtration of publick Affairs, which does not only endanger the publick Peace, as all other*
‘ *Libels do, by ſtirring up the Parties immediately concerned in it, to Acts of Revenge,*
‘ *but alſo has a direct Tendency to breed in the People a Diſlike of their Governours,*
‘ *and incline them to Faction and Sedition.* As to the 2*d*. Point he ſays, §. 10.
‘ *It is certain, not only he who compoſes or procures another to compoſe it but*
‘ *alſo that he who publiſhes, or procures another to publiſh it, are in Danger of being*
‘ *puniſhed for it; and it is ſaid not to be material whether he who diſperſes a Libel,*
‘ *knew any Thing of the Contents or Effects of it or not; for nothing could be more*

eaſy

months awaiting trial. Finally, Andrew Hamilton — Zenger's lawyer — established that since his charges were true he was not guilty of libel. Zenger went free and so did the American press.

Today all publishers are allowed by the First Amendment to publish what they choose. No government can prohibit them from so doing, though those who publish are subject to court action if they purposely damage a person's or an institution's reputation through distortions of the truth. In 1971 the federal government tried to prohibit *The New York Times* and *The Washington Post* from publishing the "Pentagon Papers," which were considered military secrets. The Supreme Court ruled that freedom of the press forbade the government to halt publication of these papers. Any legal action against a publication or a publisher can only be taken after printing since the First Amendment strictly forbids restricting material prior to publication.

Though often a center of controversy, freedom of the press is a vital part of American life. It provides citizens with issues and arguments that are never mentioned in the presses of many other countries.

The Right of Assembly and Organization

During the conflict with the colonists in America, the king of England and his governors halted some citizens' meetings in the colonies. They knew that angry colonists would stir each other up, and they wanted to prevent this. After independence was achieved, Americans remembered how important their revolutionary meetings had been. They wanted to be sure that they would always have the right to meet and to organize.

No one can change a government singlehandedly. To bring about any meaningful change, people must unite. They must meet with others and

The first page of Zenger's account of his own trial, which he published in 1736.

APRIL / MAY 1973

Rights

First amendment.

Congress shall make no law respecting an establishment of religion, or prohibiting the free exercise thereof; or abridging the freedom of speech or of the press; or the right of the people peaceably to assemble, and to petition the Government for a redress of grievances.

THIS ISSUE:

THE ADMINISTRATION'S WAR ON PRESS, RADIO, AND TV

THE NATIONAL EMERGENCY CIVIL LIBERTIES COMMITTEE

Not all demonstrations or assemblies are peaceful. At the "Boston Tea Party" colonists dressed as Indians and destroyed a large British shipment of tea.

discuss the issue concerning them, so that they can agree on a course of action. They may decide to call a public meeting or to organize a parade to arouse popular interest. They must win many followers if they are to influence or change the government. Their fight to win followers through small or large mass meetings is protected by the First Amendment.

The right of assembly and organization is closely related to the right to free speech. Thus, if a meeting is called, the police must protect it when necessary. Even if the speakers stir up the audience and they become very excited, the police must defend the right of the speakers to address the people. They may not use the excuse of an angry crowd to break up a meeting. What matters most is the right of the speakers to address the meeting.

In addition to the right to hold a meeting or a parade, the right of assembly means the right to join an organization of one's choosing. In many countries, only organizations approved by the government may hold meetings. The idea of the First Amendment is to permit any organization that does not have an immediate criminal purpose to meet and work for its goals. There are no exceptions. Communists as well as Democrats and Republicans have a Constitutional right to hold meetings. School boards can meet, and so can teachers' unions or parents' groups. Organizations dedicated to each other's ruin are all guaranteed the right to meet. However, no organization can be formed to plan a bank robbery, a kidnapping, or a murder. If such a meeting occurs, the participants can be arrested for planning to commit a crime. Even then, however, the state must prove that the meeting had a criminal purpose.

Looking at some events that have happened in our country since the First Amendment was passed, one might think that the freedom of assembly was not taken seriously. Meetings of slaves who planned to

Organizations and their publications — such as this issue of Rights, *the magazine of the National Emergency Civil Liberties Committee — are free to challenge those who are governing America.*

escape were once illegal, and participants were punished when caught. People were once arrested and imprisoned for the "conspiracy" of trying to form a trade union. But as the years passed, the American people, through their government, broadened their system of justice. People were no longer arrested for forming trade unions, for unions themselves were no longer considered illegal. And instead of treating meetings to set slaves free as criminal, the government finally declared slavery itself illegal.

The Right of Petition

The government can easily let the people know what decisions it makes and why it makes them. The president or another important government official can hold a press conference or address the nation on television. Even outside the government, certain important individuals like news commentators can let masses of people know their opinions. But how do unknown, average people let the government know how they feel about an issue? If one person's views are shared by others, they can all write and sign a petition stating their beliefs. This petition is then sent to the appropriate government official.

The government receiving the petition does not have to do what the signers request, but the government must read it. Sometimes nothing is done about the petitioners' requests, but sometimes the petition works. The basic idea in setting down grievances and gathering signatures is to show the people in power what this group of signers wants. The more people who want something, the better their chance of getting it. Politicians, like all people, want to keep their jobs. The politician who is elected must always look for voters in the next election. If a large number of people sign a certain petition, and a politician helps them to get what they ask for, the politician in turn may get their votes.

The right of petition is protected by the First Amendment. In some countries, signing a petition against an act of the government can land one in jail. In the United States, on the other hand, the government cannot penalize a person for signing a petition, no matter what it says.

The Second Amendment

In some ways, the colonists lived in a world that was very different from ours. The police could certainly not be phoned if someone were breaking into a colonist's home. Living alone on the frontier, a colonist might not even have a neighbor to yell to. Men and women had to defend homes and families by themselves, and for this they usually had a gun. If a community was invaded by armed men from another place, there was no standing army to fight off the invaders; but the colonists might have formed a militia — that is, a group of trained reservists ready to defend their community in emergencies. The Second Amendment stated that the people had the right to maintain the militia and to bear arms themselves.

Today there are regular armies, air forces, missiles, home telephones, and nearby police stations. But there are still millions of guns in the hands of individuals. One of these guns, actually a rifle, killed President John F. Kennedy. Another, a pistol, killed his brother Robert. Another rifle killed Martin Luther King. An attempt was made on the life of George Wallace with a pistol. And thousands of relatively unknown people are killed in the United States every year by individuals who have guns.

Many people, such as Senator Edward Kennedy, are saying that the country needs a strict federal gun-control law. They are saying that the Second Amendment was needed two centuries ago, but it cannot provide all the protection we need today. Others, however, say that the Second Amendment forbids the federal government to obstruct the right to bear arms, and that any such law would be unconstitutional.

Since the colonists (shown here in the Battle of Lexington) used their own guns to win independence from England, the Second Amendment protected "the right of the people to keep and bear arms."

The Third Amendment

During the days before the American Revolution, the British brought over many soldiers and officials. The British army thought nothing of requiring local people to provide rooms for their troops. While the colonists were actually British citizens themselves, they felt invaded by foreign soldiers sent to watch them. Under the Intolerable Acts, the situation grew particularly tense in Boston. British soldiers were everywhere, and the colonists were controlled by them in a military state. British officers ordered some Bostonians to provide them with meals every day, laundry service, the best bedroom, and perhaps a horse for military duty. Anyone who refused would be arrested.

The first ten amendments were written not long after these things happened. The Third Amendment stated that soldiers could not be quartered in any house, in time of peace, without the consent of the owner. Even in time of war, the government could not quarter soldiers in peoples' houses, except in a manner prescribed by law.

The Fourth Amendment

This amendment grew out of the colonists' experience with the British before and during the Revolution. British officials were trying to crack down on smuggling in the colonies. They knew that many goods had been brought illegally into the colonies, but it was often impossible to know where they were hidden. Therefore, the officials sometimes ordered many homes searched, hoping to be lucky enough to find smuggled goods in some of them. Soldiers burst into the homes of many innocent colonists during meals or in the middle of the night, ransacking the rooms and searching the people for anything they might find. They arrested and jailed many people without any real evidence against them.

To prevent their own government from ever doing these things, the writers of the Fourth Amendment prohibited "unreasonable searches and seizures" of people or their properties. The police cannot ordinarily enter your home without your permission, unless they have a specific warrant — or written certificate from the proper authorities — to do so. They cannot enter and search your home while you are away. Police cannot arrest someone unless they have good reason to suspect that that person has broken the law. While this amendment may restrict the police in their efforts to halt crimes, it protects people from arrest for little or no reason.

There are legal ways in which a home may be searched. The police may submit a list of items they are looking for to a judge, together with their reasons for believing they may be found in a certain house or building. If the judge agrees that the police have a good case, he will sign a search warrant that empowers them to search the place for the items

listed. However, if the search warrant only lists stolen furs and jewelry, the police cannot seize narcotics or other items unless they are in plain view. This prevents the police from simply hunting around for anything to incriminate a person. In like manner, a warrant for a person's arrest must name the individual and state the crime with which he or she is being charged. However, in the case of a breach of the peace or a serious crime, the police may arrest a person without a warrant.

The Fourth Amendment clearly protects you against whoever would enter your house while you were out, search your files, and copy down personal information about you. But what about wiretapping? The telephone wiretap, or the electronic "bugging" device, can, in effect, allow others to listen to your most private conversations in your own home. Generally, the courts have decided that this is illegal, even when carried out by federal agents. It invades the privacy of individuals. However, if the court decides there is a reason to suspect that illegal activities are under way that can only come to light through "bugging," it may then allow this practice.

Some have insisted that "bugging" does not violate the privacy rights because this amendment was written when there were no such things as phones or electronic devices for eavesdropping. But the Supreme Court has rejected this very permissive interpretation. And other people insist that this invasion of privacy can lead to a police state. The result of these conflicting views has been that wiretapping has generally been permitted by court order when an issue vital to the national defense or the detection of serious crime is involved. Its critics still hold that leaving this vital decision to a judge is wrong, and that no wiretapping is legal. They contend that it all invades the home and violates the Constitution.

The Fourth Amendment, which prohibits unreasonable searches and seizures, did not prevent slave-catchers from entering the homes of black people.

Fifth Amendment

The basic idea of the Fifth Amendment is to prevent injustice to those accused of crime. When people commit crimes, they are hurting others. In a country where justice prevails, the law deals with the criminal and protects the law-abiding citizen from criminal acts. Moreover, in a just country the person who is accused of a crime is protected by certain safeguards. Then, when someone's innocence or guilt is established in a fair and careful manner, people can respect the legal system.

The Fifth Amendment's first section provides that no one can be tried for a serious federal crime, such as kidnapping, unless a special jury decides to do so. This special jury is called a grand jury, and its only purpose is to see if there is enough evidence to justify bringing the accused person to trial. Because of this part of the Fifth Amendment, a sheriff cannot charge one person after another with a certain unsolved crime, and hope the regular trial jury will finally convict one of them. Trials can ruin peoples' reputations, even when they are found innocent.

If a grand jury does decide there is enough evidence against the accused person, the person is indicted, or charged with the crime. This does not mean that the accused person has been declared guilty; a person is innocent until proven guilty. But it does mean the person must stand trial. Many a person indicted by a grand jury has been found not guilty by the regular trial jury. To convince a grand jury to indict a person, a district attorney must present enough evidence to show that a trial would not be a waste of time and tax money.

Another section of the Fifth Amendment prevents the government from trying someone twice for the same crime. In days of old, if some-

The Fifth and Sixth amendments protect the accused from illegal actions by the police and other governmental agents. These are the uniforms policemen wore around 1919.

one was acquitted by a jury, an angry official could have that person arrested again and tried by another jury. This is called "double jeopardy" and it is forbidden by the Fifth Amendment. Of course, there are times when a jury cannot agree. In such cases, another trial is needed to determine a verdict. The second trial is viewed as a continuation of the first one; it is not considered a form of double jeopardy. But once the jury finds an individual innocent of a crime, that individual can never be tried again for the same crime — even if he or she later admits to it.

A difficult and controversial part of this amendment is the part that allows anyone accused of a crime to refuse to testify against oneself. Americans have a right to remain silent and say nothing that may be used against them — they may take the Fifth Amendment to protect themselves. To understand this, one has to know that in past centuries it was common practice to torture people into confessing crimes. It could easily be done today behind locked doors where there are no witnesses. People "confessing" under torture might say anything, true or untrue, just to stop their suffering. Such confessions or testimony may have no value. The Fifth Amendment was written to prevent this pointless and brutal practice.

A person may be innocent or guilty, but proof is up to others if that person wishes to remain silent. Many assume that those who do not testify against themselves in open court are guilty as accused. But an individual may remain silent to hide something very personal that is not connected to establishing guilt or innocence. During the McCarthy era of the early 1950s, many people were accused of being "Communist traitors" by members of a Senate subcommittee. The accused people could not confront their accusers, as they could have in a court trial. The senator accusing them could say anything without being sued for slander. The only protection these people had was the Fifth Amendment. They could refuse to testify against themselves by saying nothing about their politics or their friends. When some people exercised this right, Senator McCarthy called them "Fifth Amendment Communists."

Eventually, the United States Senate condemned him for conduct unbecoming to a senator.

Another vital part of the Fifth Amendment provides that no person can be denied "life, liberty, or property" without "due process of law." This means a court cannot rule that a person be executed, jailed, fined, or have personal property seized, unless the court has gone through all proper legal procedures. If all proper legal procedures are not followed, a person's conviction and punishment have to be reversed. No matter how guilty a person appears, he or she is entitled to every right of an innocent person when accused. Only when legally found guilty can a person be fined, sentenced, or denied liberty. This amendment protects people against the federal government, and it was later extended to the state governments by the Fourteenth Amendment.

The last section of the Fifth Amendment provides that whenever the government must take private land for a public purpose, it must pay the owner a fair price. Certain land is sometimes needed to build a highway, a bridge, an airstrip, or facilities that benefit many citizens. The government can force an owner of such land to sell, but it must pay the price the owner would have received on an open market. This price is set by government officials and its fairness is ruled upon by a court.

The Sixth Amendment

For thousands of years, people have been put on trial for crimes they may or may not have committed. The trial may have consisted of being tortured until they admitted committing the crime, or of being told that they were guilty by a judge who gave them little or no chance to defend themselves. People were probably resigned to this brutal treatment at the hands of the law, because it was the only kind they knew. People in the United States are guaranteed a fair trial, and the Sixth Amendment spells out what must be done if an American is charged with a crime.

First, the accused person must be given "a speedy and public trial." To insure justice, the trial must be held in public with anyone being admitted, including friends of the accused, possible victims of the accused, and even newspaper reporters. The idea behind a "speedy" trial is to prevent a person from being held in jail for a long time while the trial is being arranged However, this rule is hard to enforce because these arrangements are slowly prepared and a hasty trial would not be carefully done or, perhaps, fair. Unfortunately, many people remain in prison awaiting trial because they cannot raise the bail. Moreover, the courts have become overcrowded with cases, and each trial must wait its turn.

The accused person is also guaranteed an "impartial jury" drawn from the state and the judicial district where the crime was committed. The prospective jurors are interviewed to determine if they are free of prejudice for or against the accused. If prejudiced either way, a person is excused from this jury duty assignment. For example, a person who admitted being a pacifist might not be allowed to sit on a jury trying a military man or another pacifist. The selection of a jury is often a very slow and careful procedure, with both the prosecution and the defense having the right to examine people before they become jurors. Even with this method, a biased jury can still be selected if, for example, a black man is on trial and all of his jurors are white. Fortunately, the courts are becoming aware of this problem, and members of minority groups are now given the opportunity to serve on juries, whereas in the past they were often left out.

When a person is charged with a crime, he or she has a right to know exactly what the charge is. This charge, which is called an indictment, is put into writing so the accused can prepare a defense. If the charges are so vague that the accused cannot disprove them, the trial cannot take place.

A person on trial has the right to call witnesses to testify at the trial, and to "confront" hostile witnesses — people who are against the accused. Not only must such hostile witnesses face the person they accuse, but they must answer that person's questions in cross-examination. Dishonest testimony often falls apart when confronted with good questions. On the other hand, the accused may call supporting witnesses. Even if a witness does not wish to appear in court, the person on trial can subpoena that witness to appear. In this case, the witness must come to court and testify. The idea is to provide the defense with the same subpoena power that the government has in trying the accused.

Finally, a person on trial has a right to a lawyer. Since so many points in a trial are complicated by legal words and concepts that most people do not understand, a person needs a lawyer. This right was established long ago, but often people did not have enough money to pay a lawyer, so they simply didn't get one. A recent Supreme Court decision held that the court itself must provide lawyers for poor people on trial. Of course people can refuse to have lawyers and decide to plead their own cases. While people sometimes can plead their own cases successfully, it is considered wise to enter court with a legal expert on one's side.

The Seventh Amendment

This short amendment simply insures that in federal court a person can have a trial by a jury instead of a judge in any matter of importance to the accused. This puts the judgment in the hands of twelve jurors instead of a single judge. When the Seventh Amendment was written, people remembered how judges had been appointed by kings in Europe, or by royal governors in the colonies. A jury drawn from members of one's own community was more democratic and more likely to be fair.

The Eighth Amendment

This important amendment sets forth the limitations of bail for people awaiting trial, and fines and other punishments for people who have been convicted. The first part deals with the issue of excessive bail. The idea of bail is to insure that the person arrested will show up for trial, but not that the bail be set so high the person cannot pay it. Too high a bail keeps an individual in jail. Often the accused needs to be outside searching for witnesses and others to help in the case. However, when a person has committed a murder or another highly serious crime, allowing that person to go back out into the community might endanger other people. The accused may not be granted bail at all, or it may be set high enough to discourage escaping. Bail settings often cause great disagreement between the court and the arrested person.

The Eighth Amendment also forbids excessive fines. If one cannot pay a heavy fine, then he or she is forced to spend a specified amount of time in jail. Thus, the wealthy individual sometimes pays the fine, while the poor one committing the same crime may remain in jail. The Eighth Amendment requires that fines be reasonable — in proportion to the seriousness of the crime. Thus, a fine of $10,000 for failing to put a dime in a parking meter would certainly be "excessive."

The final part outlaws "cruel and unusual punishment." Even if a person commits a crime and is found guilty, the government cannot do anything it wishes with that person. The guilty person can be imprisoned, that is, separated from society, but not tortured. Punishments that we consider cruel and unusual were once very common. People were whipped or kept in chains, forced to labor at painful or harmful tasks,

and subjected to insulting treatment. For the most part, these barbaric punishments have disappeared in the United States. Recently the Supreme Court ruled that the death penalty is "cruel and unusual punishment" when imposed at random without standards to guide a judge or jury. This means that the government can no longer execute someone for committing a crime — at least in situations where another person guilty of the same crime may receive a lesser sentence.

States, however, can still impose the death penalty. And some state governments disagree with the Supreme Court's ruling. Many people still believe that the death penalty is needed to stop criminals. At this point in its history, America is not quite sure if the death penalty is "cruel and unusual punishment."

The Eighth Amendment protects the rights of prisoners such as these men confined on Blackwell's Island in 1875.

The Ninth Amendment

In setting forth the Bill of Rights, the founding fathers named and described certain basic rights of the people — rights that the government could not take away from them. However, they were wise enough to realize that they could not make a list of every conceivable right that Americans should have. For this reason, they wrote the Ninth Amendment. This amendment states that while some rights have been written down, these are not the only rights people have. People enjoy many other rights which the government must respect. Purposely, the amendment did not mention any of these rights. Instead, it served notice that in matters not covered specifically by the Constitution, the people and not the government automatically possess the rights.

The Tenth Amendment

The Tenth Amendment completes the Bill of Rights. It reflects the fear people had of a powerful federal government. Since the only strong government the colonists had encountered was the government of King George III, they wanted as little of this big, powerful government as possible. In 1787 transportation and communication with distant places was difficult and slow. This helped shape the fear of a strong, distant government with enormous power over their lives. There was no capital just a short jet-plane ride away, nor was one's congressman a short phone call away. The government seemed almost as far away as the British Parliament.

The fear of a powerful, distant government produced the Tenth Amendment. It stated that "powers not delegated" or given to the new government by the Constitution were held by the states or the people. Of course, powers that were delegated exclusively to the federal government, like declaring war or coining money, could not be exercised by the states. But those powers not listed by the Constitution as federal powers were automatically the powers of the state governments and the people. The only exceptions to this were the powers specifically forbidden to the states by the Constitution.

The powers automatically falling to the people or the states were not listed, leaving a broad field where the federal government could not step. This was exactly the idea of the Tenth Amendment.

The Eleventh Amendment

This amendment simply declares that no state may have a law case brought against it in a federal court by citizens of another state or of a foreign country.

Passed in 1798, it resulted from a Supreme Court case in which citizens of South Carolina sued the state of Georgia. Many people were alarmed. If this became common practice, the new nation might pull itself apart. The Eleventh Amendment ended the problem.

The Twelfth Amendment

Soon after the new government of the United States began, a flaw was discovered in the Constitution. It had to do with the way the original Constitution allowed for the election of the president and vice-president of the United States. In 1800, Thomas Jefferson and Aaron Burr were the candidates for the Republican party. Jefferson was the candidate for president and Burr for vice-president. However, the Constitution allowed the electors to vote for both men together, and the ballot did not say which one was to be president and which one to be vice-president. The result was that the seventy-three Republican electors voted seventy-three times for Jefferson and seventy-three times for Burr.

Obviously they meant to elect Jefferson president and Burr vice-president. But the vote merely showed that both men had received seventy-three votes and there was officially a tie for the presidency. Then the trouble began. Burr might have quietly stepped out of the picture. The Federalist party might have quietly stepped aside and let Jefferson be elected. This did not happen. Instead, Aaron Burr saw an opportunity to become president and the Federalists saw an opportunity to help defeat Jefferson. Since the vote was a tie, the House of Representatives had to decide whether Burr or Jefferson would become president. To defeat Jefferson, a number of Federalists planned to vote for Burr, even though he was a Republican. One man saved the day for Jefferson — his old political foe, Alexander Hamilton, a Federalist. Because Hamilton could not support his party's choice — Aaron Burr, whom he considered an evil man — he persuaded enough Federalists

to give Jefferson the needed votes. A few years later, Burr shot and killed Hamilton in a duel.

It was necessary to make sure this kind of electoral mistake never happened again. To insure that a presidential and vice-presidential candidate did not tie or get mixed up again, a new amendment was needed. The Twelfth Amendment was passed in 1804 and provided that each office be elected separately. Although two names appear on our ballots today, they are clearly designated as president and vice-president.

Thomas Jefferson, third president of the United States, is remembered for the humane and liberal attitudes he brought to a powerful office. Jefferson emphasized strong local government, and fiercely opposed any forms of tyranny.

The Thirteenth Amendment

During the long colonial period of American history, captured Africans and their descendants worked for their entire lives as slaves owned by other people. The colonial period of our history ended with the Declaration of Independence, which stated that all men were created equal and that the United States was an independent nation. The new nation adopted a Constitution and added to it a Bill of Rights guaranteeing Americans basic liberties described in the preceding pages. The world admired the great strides toward democracy and fair play that the new nation was taking. But some people asked, how can they do all this and still keep people as slaves?

At long last, after the Civil War ended with the defeat of the South, the government that once passed the Bill of Rights finally ended slavery. The Thirteenth Amendment was ratified in 1865, but it did not and does not create social and political equality for all people of the country. It simply states that slavery is illegal in the United States.

This was the first of three amendments that were passed to alleviate problems resulting from the Civil War. The next two amendments grew from the need to protect ex-slaves and their new freedom.

Above, slavery was abolished by the Thirteenth Amendment. Below, President Lincoln informs his Cabinet that he intends to issue the Emancipation Proclamation freeing the slaves in Confederate territory. It was only a war measure and had to be made final by the Thirteenth Amendment.

The Fourteenth Amendment pledged equal rights to the ex-slaves. This school run by blacks in Charleston, South Carolina, was held in a room where blacks had been sold as slaves only a few months earlier.

The Fourteenth Amendment

Perhaps no amendment since the Bill of Rights has had a more significant impact on America than the Fourteenth Amendment. Passed in 1868, it sought to deal with the outrageous violations of the rights of ex-slaves, but it has touched on very different subjects in its long history. Although very important, its original intent to insure the rights of former slaves had little to do with its eventual effect.

In the first years after the Civil War, the South was aflame with violence toward ex-slaves and Yankee sympathizers. The Rebel spirit had not died at Appomattox, but surged forward. Instead of the old "slave codes" to control blacks, new "black codes" accomplished the same end. Blacks were not allowed to own property, to stay out at night beyond a curfew, to be without a job, to vote, to sit on a jury, or to sue white people. About the only right granted to the former slaves was the right to a legal marriage. With the laws of the South clearly on their side, bands of southern whites shot blacks on sight or drove successful black farmers off their farms so they could seize their crops. Meetings of black people, even in schools and churches, were under constant violent attack.

The federal government reacted. Congress passed the Fourteenth Amendment and it was ratified. The first section made black citizens equal to all citizens in their home states. As people who had been born in this country, they were declared citizens of the United States as well. The states were forbidden to deny blacks the rights granted to whites. Since equality under the law was the keynote of this section, the "black codes" and other discriminatory laws were prohibited. A decade before this amendment, the Supreme Court had called black people "property" with no rights; now it called them full citizens. And, for the first time, the Constitution with its Bill of Rights was made to deal with state governments as well as the federal government.

Tragically, this much-needed section of the Fourteenth Amendment soon fell into disuse. Its aim of protecting the rights of black people faded as the federal government lost interest in this matter. The country was growing fast and industry was expanding by leaps and bounds. The Supreme Court began to apply the Fourteenth Amendment to the rights of a new "person," the corporation. Since states could not deprive "any person" of "life, liberty, or property without due process of law," giant corporations found protection in this amendment. While the rights of corporations were being increasingly protected, white supremacy governments returned to the southern states. The Ku Klux Klan rode again, using violence to suppress blacks. Black rights were destroyed despite this amendment.

In 1883 the Supreme Court ruled that an 1875 civil rights law was unconstitutional. The law had done little more than carry forth the intention of the first part of the Fourteenth Amendment. In 1896 the Supreme Court again decided to ignore the amendment. It allowed a law to pass requiring black and white people to occupy different sections of railroad trains. This was not discrimination, said a majority of the Court, but a convenience for both races. The accommodations were "separate but equal." Soon more facilities such as schools, public bathrooms, and others just became segregated. The impact upon Americans of this total disregard of part of the Constitution was great. Even when equal rights were written into the Constitution, whites discriminated against blacks.

Recently this section of the Fourteenth Amendment has been given new life. In 1954 the Supreme Court ruled that segregated schools and other public facilities were unconstitutional. Further, the "due process of law" section has given more rights to poor people accused of crimes and people on welfare.

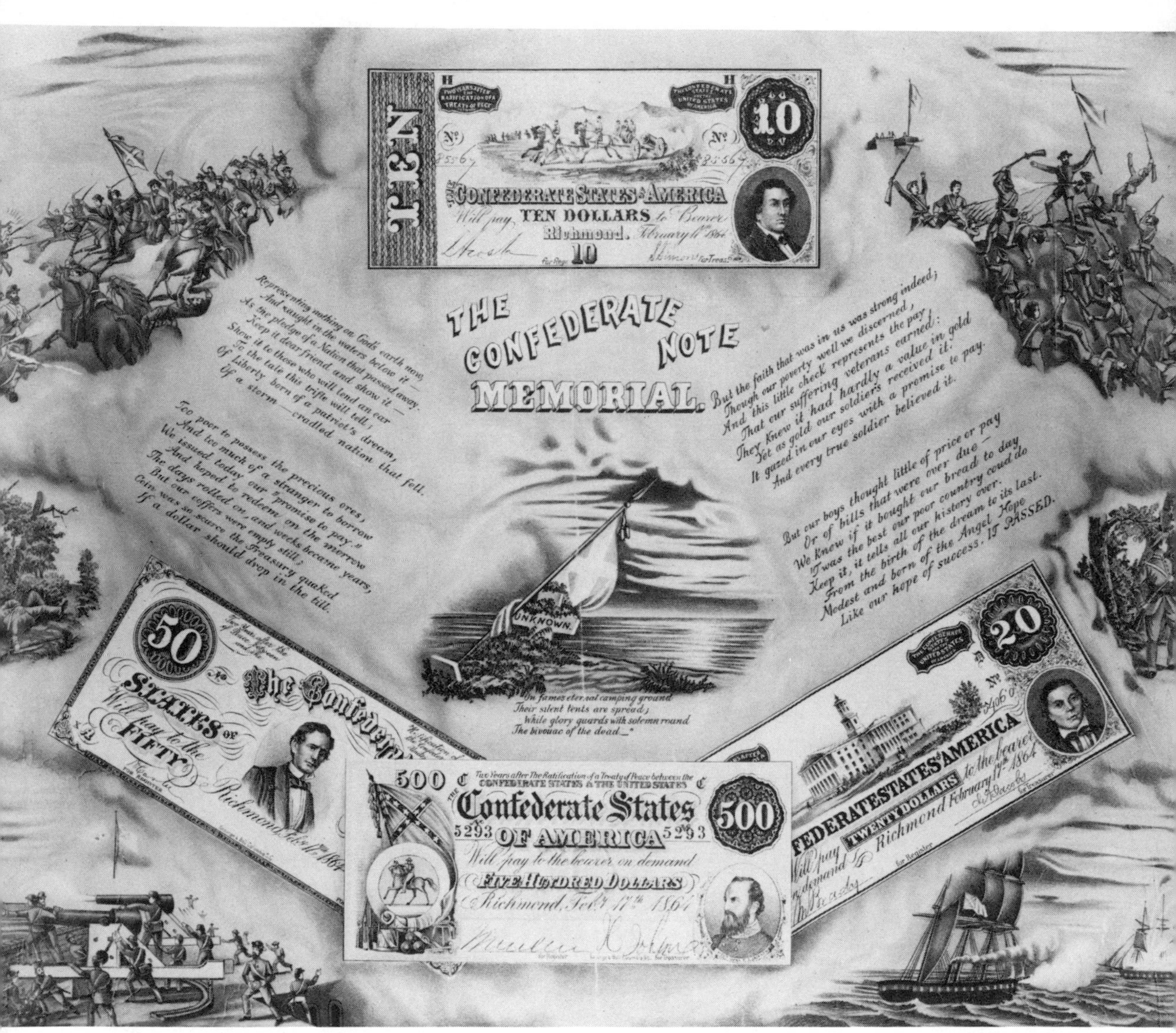

The final sections of the Fourteenth Amendment forbade payment of the Confederate debts or monies such as these paper bills.

The second section of the Fourteenth Amendment sought to provide a way of making sure it would be enforced. If a state limited anyone's right to vote, its number of representatives in Congress would be cut down according to how much of the vote was limited. This was a direct way of insuring that the ex-slaves could vote. If half of the adult males in a southern state were denied the right to vote because of their color, half of the state's congressmen would lose their jobs. This provision, clear as it is, has never been enforced.

The third and fourth sections of the amendment prohibit those who were leaders during the Confederate rebellion from holding federal or state office. The United States and the individual states are also forbidden to pay the war debts of the old Confederacy. These punishments of the Confederate war leaders have faded into the distant past. The problem of equal citizenship for all Americans has not.

The Fifteenth Amendment

By 1870 when this amendment was passed, violence against black voters and their friends was at a high point in the southern states. Congressional investigations revealed that the Ku Klux Klan and other white supremacy organizations designed raids to destroy black voting power. When black victims took their grievances to court, they found that Klansmen dominated the juries and even served as judges. In these courts convictions of the white raiders were impossible, and even indictments were unlikely.

The Fifteenth Amendment was a legal way to deal with those bent on preventing blacks from voting. It simply affirmed that no one can be denied the right to vote because of his race, color, or former slave status. Once again, like the Fourteenth Amendment, this one was violated more than obeyed. In 1877 the last of the federal troops enforcing Reconstruction were removed from the South. Now blacks were increasingly driven away from the polls and from public office. In the early 1870s, as many as eight black men served in the U.S. Congress. By the 1890s, it was down to one, and after 1901 it was none.

The Fifteenth Amendment stands again as proof that no matter how securely black rights are written into law, they may not be enforced if whites are unwilling. After Reconstruction, the North and the South began to be reconciled. The United States began to forget the enmity, bitterness, and killing of the Civil War. The ex-slaves were also forgotten. It seemed easier for the North and the South to draw together again if the Fourteenth and Fifteenth amendments were simply not enforced. Until the Voting Rights Act of 1965 was passed a century

later, this issue remained a dead letter. It came alive again only because of the drive of black Americans for their full civil rights, and a recognition by other Americans that justice could no longer be delayed.

The heroism of black troops during the Civil War, such as these in North Carolina liberating slaves in 1864, helped convince the nation that black men should have the right to vote.

The Sixteenth Amendment

The decades following the Civil War saw a tremendous industrial outburst. The United States was rapidly changing into the country we know today. The nation, which had been mainly agricultural, was becoming mostly industrial. The old hero had been the frontiersman who tamed the wilderness. The new hero was the hard-driving, financial genius who manipulated stocks, bought and sold properties, and made a fortune on the weaknesses of others. There were few laws to interfere with him, since the government felt that the economy worked better if left alone.

However, not everyone was happy with the new hero. There was a sharp reaction against the building of personal fortunes on the misfortunes of others. The Populist party of the 1890s united the farmer and the factory worker against the eastern banker and the industrialist. In an age when the emphasis was put on making a fortune with little concern for how this was accomplished, both millionaires and paupers increased in the nation. The Populists demanded that wealth be shared by all, including the poor. They proposed a series of reforms to save the farmer from creditors, to save the worker from ruthless employers, and to keep the poor from starving to death in the midst of plenty.

One of their proposals was a federal tax on everyone's income. Today the income tax is so familiar that it is difficult to imagine how radical this proposal sounded when the Populists suggested it. Since the Constitution forbade this kind of direct federal tax, it required an amendment. The people who favored it felt that everyone should pay for the nation's expenses, and those who had more money should pay more.

As rich people became richer and paid no tax on their wealth, the demand rose for an income tax.

Opponents called it socialistic because it placed a heavier burden on the rich. In 1913, the Sixteenth Amendment passed, allowing Congress to pass laws taxing incomes. Today, income tax reform is still a lively topic. The emphasis now is usually on altering the law to make sure the rich do not escape their responsibilities through "loopholes" in current laws.

The Seventeenth Amendment

During the age of aggressive businessmen and industrial growth, Americans frequently found themselves infuriated by Congress's failure to protect the public. Putrid meats and dangerous drugs were sold to the consumer. Even candy sold to children sometimes contained harmful impurities. Yet Congress seemed unwilling to do anything about this.

Writers known as "muckrakers" pointed out that various senators and congressmen were controlled by major corporations. Articles in popular magazines called the Senate "the millionaires' club" because so many of its members were wealthy, or were chosen by wealthy people. The muckrakers even referred to "the treason of the Senate." This may have been strong language, but one thing is certain: the senators were not elected by the people.

The original Constitution provided that the various state legislatures choose the United States Senate. Therefore, the legislature of each state picked the two senators for that state. This allowed men who were not popular to win simply by convincing enough legislators to vote for them. It was charged that sometimes senators were selected on the basis of favors or bribes.

The Populist party of the 1890s and other reformers repeatedly asked for a popular Senate. By this they meant that senators should not be chosen by the legislatures, but elected by the people. They felt that the senator who bribed a few legislators for his job could never make it in an open appeal to the voters.

Finally, in 1913, the Seventeenth Amendment was ratified. The U.S. Senate was to be elected by the people in their respective states, as was

The United States Senate had become "the millionaire's club, dominated by powerful economic interests." Note that the "Peoples' Entrance" is closed and locked in this 1889 cartoon.

the House of Representatives. But a woman could not run for the Senate until the women's rights movement brought about ratification of the Nineteenth Amendment.

Today the Seventeenth Amendment is not in dispute, since all agree it has moved the nation toward greater democracy. Some reformers have pointed out that it has not worked perfectly. A man can still be elected senator more easily than another if he has more money to spend. He can often win his party's nomination and the election itself if his campaign is well financed. But unlike candidates before the Seventeeth Amendment, he still has to win the votes of the people to be elected.

The Eighteenth Amendment

This amendment has the dubious distinction of being the only one ever repealed by another amendment. But in 1919, when the Eighteenth Amendment was ratified by the states, many people thought that it was a fine thing for the country and long overdue. It forbade the manufacture and sale of alcoholic beverages in the United States.

If it is acceptable today for adults to drink alcoholic beverages in moderation, why was this amendment even considered back in 1919? A long and vigorous campaign had pointed to heavy drinking as a major American sickness. Stories, novels, and plays dealt with the working man on the way home to his family, stopping off at the neighborhood bar. A few drinks and some conversation lead to a fight and more drinking. When he finally reaches his home, the family discovers that their drunken father has spent the whole week's wages. No money for rent, clothing for the children, or even food.

A powerful organization known as the Women's Christian Temperance Union (WCTU) sparked the campaign to ban drinking. Some of its militant officers marched into bars and swung axes at kegs of beer.

Above, this illustration from The Bottle and the Pledge, *an early temperance tale about the evils of drink, shows the destruction of a happy home as a husband gives liquor to his wife. Below, this 1901 cartoon shows Carry Nation, a militant leader of the Women's Christian Temperance Union (WCTU), after one of her antidrinking "campaigns."*

MRS NATION

Others threw bricks through saloon windows. Some canvassed their congressmen advocating an amendment to ban the manufacture and sale of "demon rum."

The movement grew stronger with the approach of World War I. Here was a nation preparing to "make the world safe for democracy." How could it march into battle drunk? Besides, so many breweries, some pointed out, were owned by Germans, and Germany was an enemy in that war. Nationalist feeling merged with a popular fear of the evils of drinking. It soon became unsafe for politicians to oppose Prohibition. They were made to appear as though they favored sin, or did not care if men drank away their families' money. In 1919, the Eighteenth Amendment was ratified and it made newspaper headlines all over the world.

The Nineteenth Amendment

When the Constitution was written and the Bill of Rights added, no one suggested that equality applied to women. The early laws of the republic actually considered women the property or wards of their fathers or husbands. In some places women could not own property and had little legal control over their children. If he wanted to, a man could marry and divorce one woman after another and walk off lightheartedly with the property and the children of each victim.

In the midst of the abolitionist agitation against slavery, a strong women's rights movement also got under way. In 1848, a women's convention held at Seneca Falls, New York, became the first to demand the right to vote for women. This idea was greeted with laughter by men throughout the country. Women's place is in the home, they said. They praised their wives and mothers as wonderful women, vital to the family. But the idea of their wives voting just like men was ridiculous. Their wives usually agreed.

However, the women's rights campaign did not cease. Elizabeth Cady Stanton was arrested and jailed for voting in the 1870s. She conducted her own trial with dignity and courage, but she was still found guilty of violating the law. A few states in the West finally began to grant women's suffrage, but others voted it down emphatically. It was clear that if women were ever to win the elementary right to vote, a new Constitutional amendment was needed.

Women's rights organizations increased the pressure on government. Demonstrations and petitions flooded the halls of Congress demanding votes for women, and the Nineteenth Amendment providing women's

suffrage was proposed. Noting that the United States had just entered a war "to make the world safe for democracy," President Woodrow Wilson called on legislators to pass the amendment. By 1920 the Nineteenth Amendment had passed and women voted in the presidential election of that year. For the first time in the history of the republic, women had a choice in the selection of those who made laws for them.

Women demanded the right to vote long before they finally won it in 1919.

The Twentieth Amendment

Before the Twentieth Amendment was passed in 1933, people used to joke grimly about "lame duck" presidents or congressmen. Although presidents and congressmen were elected in November, the president-elect did not take office until March 4, and the congressmen did not start until the *following December*, thirteen months after election. Meanwhile, the "lame ducks," still in power but waiting to retire, had nothing to lose by doing very little. The newly elected representatives of the people were unable to do anything until their long wait was over.

Perhaps the most dramatic instance of this occurred after the election of President Abraham Lincoln. The Southern states then began to secede from the United States while the president-elect waited months for his inauguration. President Buchanan, Lincoln's predecessor, was later charged with aiding the secession movement during his "lame duck" days. In early 1933, just before the Twentieth Amendment finally passed, the country was entering another time of crisis requiring strong presidential action. A nation-wide depression stalked the land throwing millions out of jobs and into bread lines. Misery and desperation grew in every town.

When Franklin D. Roosevelt came to power, his first hundred days were filled with strong and far-reaching acts to halt the decline of economic strength in America. It was clear that never again should an

On March 4, 1861, President-elect Abraham Lincoln, accompanied by President Buchanan, proceeds down Pennsylvania Avenue to the Capitol Building for his inauguration.

BOOK SALE

American Congress or president have to wait for a long time before assuming the office to which they had been elected. The Twentieth Amendment passed the same year, and it required that a new president elected in November take office January 20 instead of March 4. It also required senators and representatives elected in November to take office January 3, instead of waiting for another whole year. The need for this sort of rapid transfer of power today, in an age of missiles and jets, is clearer than ever.

The Twenty-first Amendment

This amendment simply repealed the Eighteenth Amendment that had prohibited the manufacture and sale of alcoholic drinks. What had happened in the dozen years of Prohibition that led to repeal?

First, the nation experienced the manufacture and consumption of alcoholic drinks on a larger scale than ever before. Illegal "speakeasies" appeared in every large city in the United States. People flocked to them to drink with their friends and hear the jazz music that swept the nation. It seemed that the forbidding of alcoholic drinks had merely stimulated a desire for them. In other words, the "noble experiment" to ban drinking in America by changing the Constitution had failed miserably.

But Prohibition had done even worse than that to the country. Since liquor could not be manufactured and sold legitimately, this business was left to those willing to engage in it as a criminal act. Gangsters quickly dominated the illegal industry. In Chicago, Al Capone symbolized the new power of gangsters who now controlled an important American business. The police forces of major cities were kept busy trying to contain a huge crime wave created by Prohibition.

All this meant that during the era of Prohibition, Americans experienced a period of lawlessness, one that openly flouted the United States Constitution. Both prominent and ordinary people participated in drinking, and everyone was aware of this illegal national pastime. Prohibition had really done nothing for America but increase violations of and disrepect for the law. It also added to the number of criminals at work.

When the stock market crashed in 1929, and the Great Depression forced millions out of work, the illicit glamor of the Roaring Twenties died. The total failure of Prohibition seemed more clear, and many voices demanded a saner approach to alcohol consumption. The Twenty-first Amendment was passed in 1933 and Prohibition's "noble experiment" was ended.

Americans found many ways of getting around the Prohibition Law.

The Twenty-second Amendment

When George Washington retired from the presidency, he told Americans that no one should hold that office for more than two terms. The first president knew that those who stay at the center of power too long tend to cling to that power. Well-entrenched governments become rigid and opposed to change. In short, they become dictatorial. If a government becomes a dictatorship, it can only be changed by revolution. For a century and a half after Washington's famous statement, no president held office for more than two terms.

This tradition was broken by Franklin D. Roosevelt. In 1932, and again in 1936, 1940, and 1944 he was elected to the presidency. People were impressed with his way of handling two great crises — the Great Depression and then the American role in World War II. The slogan of the time was "Don't change horses in midstream," and the country reelected President Roosevelt to a third and even a fourth term.

The Twenty-second Amendment arose from delayed anger toward President Roosevelt and some of his policies. The Republican party, which he had defeated four times at the polls, tended to speak of his time in office as an undemocratic seizure of power. They proposed the amendment to limit a president to two terms. It gained wide national support and passed in 1951. As it reads, this amendment restricts a president to two full terms. If a vice-president assumes the presidency

The Twenty-second Amendment prevented any president from serving more than two terms. It was a reaction to the four terms of New Deal President Franklin D. Roosevelt.

on the death of a president before two years are up, he can only run for election once. Vice-President Lyndon Johnson became president upon the assassination of President John F. Kennedy. Because Johnson had then served less than two years as president, he could have run twice more for the office if he had chosen to. At this point in history, the amendment has not restricted any president, for none has indicated a desire to serve more than two terms.

The Twenty-third Amendment

Washington, D.C., the seat of the federal government, has long had a population that includes many federal employees. Until recently, it was considered unwise to let these people vote. As federal employees, they could easily be guided to vote for the party that provided their jobs. This was especially true in the nineteenth century when the ballot was not secret. Forbidding the residents of the capital to vote was actually considered a reform, a means to prevent fraud and pressure to surrender votes.

However, changes brought about a need for new thinking. The secret ballot was introduced for voters all over the United States. The population of Washington, D.C., grew to include not merely federal employees but many other citizens. Yet none of them had the right to vote, and this city was the capital of the United States! A further aggravation was that the government of this metropolis was run by a committee of Congress. Here was a prize example of undemocratic procedure: a congressional committee not elected by the people of the district setting its rules and taxes.

The Twenty-third Amendment has sought to remedy this injustice to the people living in the nation's capital. It authorized Washington, D.C., residents to vote for candidates for president and vice-president of the United States. Congress then passed legislation granting the District its own local government. Its first mayor, Walter Washington, was appointed by President Lyndon Johnson, a Democrat, and reappointed by President Richard Nixon, a Republican. This was an attempt to accept the residents' wishes, because Mayor Washington and 80 per-

cent of the District's inhabitants are blacks. The Twenty-third Amendment illustrates how a constitutional change can lead to other reform legislation.

Walter Washington, first mayor of the nation's capital.

The Twenty-fourth Amendment

Starting in colonial times, one method of restricting voting was the poll tax. This was simply a government tax on a person allowed to vote. This tax was undemocratic because it hindered people from voting. Since the rich could more easily pay the tax than the poor, it became a means of limiting the number of poor voters. Poll taxes were often scheduled for collection just before people voted — reason enough to keep many from voting.

After emancipation, southern states used the poll tax as a major weapon for reducing the number of black voters at the polls. Most blacks in the South from the Civil War to World War II were employed on farms as sharecroppers. Their expenses were deducted from their wages or crops, and the records of all this were kept by the landlord. Most sharecroppers found at the end of each season that, according to their white landlord, they had either earned no money or had actually gone into debt. There was no point in taking the landlord to court, since the court was dominated by unsympathetic whites.

Poor whites throughout the South also suffered from the poll tax, since it discriminated against poor people regardless of color. A tax for voting might amount to two dollars a year, but for a person with a

The Twenty-fourth Amendment prevents states from charging voters a poll tax. For years the poll tax kept blacks and poor whites, like these miners, from voting.

family to support and little cash, this was an enormous amount to pay merely for voting. In addition, the tax was cumulative. If someone failed to pay it for several years and then went to vote, he was presented with a bill for the years the tax had not been paid.

The impact of the poll tax on southern voting was heavy. In states such as New York and Pennsylvania it might take one hundred thousand voters to elect a congressman, while in Mississippi or Alabama it took only five or ten thousand. With such a small group privileged to vote, some southern congressmen owed their election or reelection to a very small number of voters. They could ignore the masses of potential voters who were kept away by the poll tax.

The Twenty-fourth Amendment ended the poll tax or any other tax as a requirement for voting. It was passed in 1964, aided by the growing importance of the civil rights movement at that time.

The Twenty-fifth Amendment

This amendment answered questions that had troubled government leaders for many years. Suppose the president were stricken by an illness or an assassination attempt that left him alive but incapable of doing his job? And worse, suppose he didn't realize how ill he was and continued to hold office? The United States could then be governed by a man whose judgment was badly impaired. This was too terrifying a prospect in a world of superpowers and nuclear weapons.

Is this kind of concern melodramatic? History suggests it is not. From 1900 until the year this amendment passed, 1967, the United States had twelve presidents. Four of them died in office, two by assassination. Others were seriously ill, such as President Wilson who suffered a paralyzing stroke, while occupying the White House. Until the passage of the Twenty-fifth Amendment, it was entirely possible for a president to remain at the head of government even though his judgment and understanding were gravely damaged. Even if a president recognized his disability and wanted the vice-president to take over until his recovery, the original Constitution did not clearly allow this to be done.

Under the Twenty-fifth Amendment, the president can temporarily turn his office over to the vice-president by writing to the heads of the Senate and House informing them of his disability. Then, the vice-president becomes acting president until the president writes another letter announcing he is able to return to office.

If, however, the president is incapacitated and does not know or admit it, a more complicated method must be followed. The vice-president and a majority of the heads of the executive departments — members of the Cabinet — must write to the heads of the Senate and

the House stating that the president is unable to carry out his duties. Then, the vice-president immediately assumes the office of acting president. But, if and when the president writes to the Senate and House leaders that "no inability exists," he then resumes his office. However, if the vice-president and a majority of the Cabinet members are still persuaded that the president is unable to function, they must write the Senate and House leaders to this effect within four days. At this point, the confrontation is complete. Congress must now decide who is to be president of the United States!

This Amendment filled another gap in the Constitution. When the office of the vice-president is empty, the president must nominate a vice-president who takes office with the approval of Congress. The Twenty-fifth Amendment safeguards against the kind of brutal power struggle that has scarred less fortunate countries.

In October of 1973 this amendment was used for the first time. Vice-President Spiro T. Agnew resigned and pleaded guilty to a charge in federal court. President Nixon selected Congressman Gerald Ford to succeed Agnew as vice-president. Congress then met and approved the nomination of Ford as the new vice-president of the United States.

President Woodrow Wilson, disabled by a stroke after World War I, proved that something had to be done about a president who could not function in office. The Twenty-fifth Amendment, passed in the wake of President John F. Kennedy's assassination, sought to deal with this difficult situation.

The Twenty-sixth Amendment

Nothing is more necessary for democracy than the right to vote. By voting, the people actually control their government. They can decide which officials shall remain in power. They can also decide who shall leave public office and by whom they shall be replaced. They can vote for lawmakers who are liberal or conservative, thereby shaping the laws that are subsequently passed. They can vote on propositions that determine how their taxes are to be spent. Voters have a deep responsibility for the kind of officials they put in office. Eligible people who do not vote have an equal responsibility, since their inaction means that a smaller number of voters will choose the government for everybody.

Until the Twenty-sixth Amendment was passed in 1971, most states required that voters be at least twenty-one years of age. Yet eighteen-year-olds have worked, paid taxes, married, and supported families. They have been called into military service, and they have fought and died in wars. Yet they could not vote for or against those who controlled their very lives.

Agitation for the vote for eighteen-year-olds grew in recent years. The Vietnam War, the nation's longest and most controversial war, sharpened public awareness of the exploitation of young Americans. Youth movements, protesting the system we live by, shocked older voters into facing certain realities. The young dissenters could hardly take their grievances from the streets to the polls if they were not allowed to vote. The Twenty-sixth Amendment reduced the voting age to eighteen.

Because so many young men lost their lives in the Vietnam War, the Twenty-sixth Amendment (passed in 1971) lowered the voting age from twenty-one to eighteen.

These women clothing workers braving a Chicago snowfall in 1910 demonstrated their refusal to accept unfair wages and unsafe working conditions. Americans continue to demonstrate for change and new rights under the Constitution.

Conclusion

Through the years the Constitution of the United States has changed with the times. The process of amendments has allowed for many of the greatest changes of all. Generally, the new additions have provided citizens with greater rights. Voting, once restricted to a rich few, now reaches to groups it never touched before — women, those under twenty-one, the poor, and the minorities.

Those who seek to change the government one way or another still have the opportunity to change its basic law, the Constitution. The process of passing an amendment is slow and difficult, but this is to prevent passage of hastily conceived ideas in a rash of emotional enthusiasm. This did happen once, despite the slow processes, with the passage of the Eighteenth Amendment prohibiting the manufacture and sale of liquor. This was finally repealed with passage of the Twenty-first Amendment. But even this action proved the workability of the Constitution, which was initially designed to reinforce liberty rather than restrict it.

Today many citizens talk of amending the Constitution to provide for new situations. As this is written, another amendment is being considered by the states. The Equal Rights Amendment provides for complete equality of female and male citizens in all phases of American life. Others have talked of altering the Constitution to provide for strict control of guns, to prevent bussing of children to integrate schools, and for a variety of other purposes. Only the people, by voting, can decide whether these will become part of the law of the land.

Bibliography

Belasco, Milton J., and Hammond, Harold Earl. ". . . *A More Perfect Union": The Constitution of the United States.* New York: Washington Square Press, 1966.

Douglas, William O. *A Living Bill of Rights.* New York: Anti-Defamation League of B'nai B'rith, 1961.

Findlay, Bruce and Esther. *Your Rugged Constitution.* Stanford, Calif.: Stanford University Press, 1952.

Meltzer, Milton. *The Right to Remain Silent.* New York: Harcourt Brace Jovanovich, Inc., 1972.

Morris, Richard B. *The First Book of the Constitution.* New York: Franklin Watts, Inc., 1958.

Padover, Saul K. *The Living U.S. Constitution.* New York: Mentor Books, 1954.

Tresolini, Rocco J., ed. *Constitutional Decisions in American Government.* New York: Macmillan, 1965.

About the Constitution. New York: National Emergency Civil Liberties Committee, 1972.

Equal Justice Under Law: The Supreme Court In American Life. Washington, D.C.: The Foundation of the Federal Bar Association, 1965.

Index

About the Authors

For fifteen years, William Loren Katz has taught United States history to high school students. He has served as a consultant to state departments of education and to the Smithsonian Institution. He is presently Consulting Editor for a series of picture albums on ethnic minority groups in America today and author of *A Picture Album of the Civil War,* both published by Franklin Watts, Inc.

His other works include the award-winning *Eyewitness: The Negro in American History* (1967); *American Majorities and Minorities* (1970); and *The Black West: A Documentary and Pictorial History* (1971). Mr. Katz is presently working on several other books to be published by Franklin Watts, Inc.: *An Album of Reconstruction; A History of Ethnic Minority Groups in America* (6 volumes); and a study of *Violence in America.* Mr. Katz lives in New York City and is currently a scholar-in-residence at Teachers College, Columbia University.

Mr. Bernard Gaughran has taught high school social studies for fifteen years. He is presently a consultant to several different school systems in the state of New York.